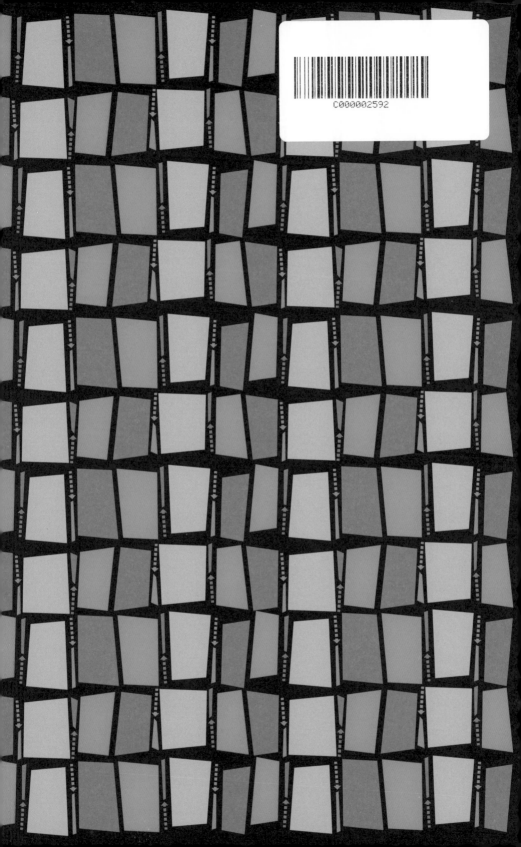

Brian Cue

On the Snap

THREE DECADES OF SNAPSHOTS
FROM THE WORLD OF JAZZ,
FILM & CRIME FICTION

On the Snap

THREE DECADES OF SNAPSHOTS
FROM THE WORLD OF JAZZ,
FILM & CRIME FICTION

BY BRIAN CASE

Caught by the River

Foreword

BY RICHARD WILLIAMS

L IKE a great improviser, Brian Case veers away from the changes in order to find the phrase he needs. He's listening to Johnny Griffin burning off the opposition at a ludicrously fast tempo. 'Re-entry goggles all round!' That's all you need. You're there, senses heightened. For his readers, Brian made the bar in Ronnie Scott's feel like the Algonquin round table.

His name was the first on my list back in 1978 when I found myself in a new editing job at the *Melody Maker* and with the chance to assemble a dream team. Persuading him to come over from the opposition constituted a major coup.

Dreaming up an assignment for Brian was the pleasure I always knew it would be, but the experience of receiving the completed article was even better: about as good, in fact, as an editor's life gets, sitting back with the typescript or printout and enjoying the experience of having your expectations exceeded, and knowing your readers will feel the same. With Brian, it happened on a weekly basis.

He had a reputation as a stylist, which can be a euphemism for sins committed in the name of creativity. But his writing was surprising, funny, allusive, erudite, emotionally engaged, every paragraph containing an unexpected verbal firecracker, all stitched together with a degree of care and craftsmanship that shaped the narrative and sustained its drive.

Here he describes a much-anticipated London debut by the saxophonist Art Pepper, which took place in a packed Hammersmith church in 1979: 'The biting silver of his alto flashed among the gilt crucifixes, the lyrical ache at the core of his soul rushed upwards along the massive granite aspiration of the nave. Architectures locked like fists, the one a frozen perfection of forgotten quarries, hoists and blueprints, the other living, precarious, transient...' No styling there: just a gift for the cadence of words, for precise observation, with an instinct for teasing truth from the connections.

When I approached him, he'd spent a couple of years at the *New Musical Express,* founded in 1952 as a pop weekly. His arrival there, at the invitation of the great Nick Logan, coincided with a wholesale revamp that would go on to embrace the punk rebellion and its offshoots. Brian was twice as old as some of their writers, more than twice as wise, and several times cooler. They spotted that and gave him due respect. He had published a first novel, *The Users,* in 1968, earning an encomium from Anthony Burgess that read like a wine expert's summary ('sexy without being lubricious, tough, witty, with a very palatable astringency'), but his pieces in the *NME* helped widen a late-blooming reputation.

He came over to the *Melody Maker* partly because I was offering to replace his freelance life at the *NME* with the security of a staff job but also, I think, because the *MM* had been started in 1926 as a journal for dance-band musicians and had evolved as a paper with jazz at its core. He was coming to a place where everyone knew how to spell 'Thelonious' and he would not be required to explain a desire to interview Art Pepper.

And it would bring him into contact with Max Jones, the doyen of the paper's jazz coverage. A former dance-band saxophonist, Max was then in his early sixties, having joined the paper in 1944. He could count entire generations of great musicians, including Louis Armstrong and (until her death) Billie Holiday, among his friends. Brian and Max bonded immediately, each seeing in the other's presence a reassurance that jazz would retain its space in the paper. Brian christened Max the Senior Beret (Jones did indeed wear one, to disguise the result of an overnight loss of hair some decades earlier) and referred to himself, in more metaphorical terms, as the Junior Beret. It fitted perfectly.

What a great time it was, although it couldn't last for ever. I'm not sure I ever had a happier week as an editor than the one in which I asked Brian to put together a piece celebrating the 20th anniversary of Ronnie Scott's; he came back – having talked to Ronnie, his business partner Pete King, Fat Henry, the cloakroom attendant who became Ben Webster's bosom pal and protector, and Jimmy Parsons, the maitre d', who might or might not have been the one who turned Miles Davis away from the door one busy Soho night –

with something that got to the essence of a precious but outwardly forbidding institution.

Typecasting was occasionally a danger. 'Writing about fallen angels is schtick,' he says in this book, but of course it was sometimes too tempting an opportunity for an editor to ignore. Pepper was one, and the result was a classic. And if Brian didn't admire Chet Baker, he would still hang with the trumpeter long enough to produce a marvellously observed piece. Left to himself, he approached musicians not with a sentimentally romanticised vision of who they were or might be, but with a sympathetic understanding of what they had been through. They responded to that. Dexter Gordon, Art Blakey and others gave him the stuff from which he could fashion great copy.

And he knew how to listen around the edges, too. I remember him coming back and saying that an English pianist who'd been playing with Johnny Griffin had related to him the tenorist's tersely abbreviated instruction for a three-tune set: 'Things, leaves, blues.' The Enigma machine inside a bebopper's head knew how to break that code to reveal the harmonic steeplechase of 'All the Things You Are' followed by the ballad 'Autumn Leaves' and a concluding 12-bar. That was the secret language of an endangered species, and Brian loved it.

He moved on to *Time Out*, where he interviewed film actors, Magnum photographers and crime and literary novelists while also editing the books page, and showed himself to be terrific in both dimensions. All his subjects, from Ian Dury to Norman Mailer, from Don McCullin to Tom Waits, the whole gang of motormouths and shutterbugs, junkies and pussy hounds, the witnesses to bebop and Belsen, get a fair hearing and words shaped by an acute sensibility. And if Al Pacino ever reads the description of the time he was interviewed by Brian Case, who happened to be carrying a hundred live bullets from his grandfather's Colt 45 in the pockets of his trenchcoat that day, he won't need to reach back for whatever Lee Strasberg taught him about how to laugh.

Richard Williams.

RICHARD WILLIAMS, 2015

Introduction

BY JAMES OLDHAM

OVER eight decades, Brian Case – son of a Deptford cop and lifelong jazzer – has been and done a lot of things but I doubt you recognize the name.

He's roamed the Fourth Estate rapping out angular prose for *NME*, *The Times*, *Uncut* and *Time Out* among many others. He's been a critically acclaimed author (his 1968 novel *The Users* – a violent existential English bebop farce – was critically lauded and endorsed by Anthony Burgess). And for anyone who's ever come across him he's been the guide to an underground, after-midnight landscape of book, film and music.

The ride has certainly been a colourful one. He's taken live ammo to an Al Pacino interview, wrestled Will Self to the floor at a book launch and abruptly curtailed a Burt Lancaster press conference by calling him Mr Reynolds.

That's before we even mention him taking horse tranquilizers in the States with Ian Dury, reluctantly hitting the road with the Sex Pistols on their first UK tour ('Idiots!') and interviewing Miles Davis in a totally blacked-out room ('I didn't interview Miles, I interviewed his voice.').

Throughout his lifetime, he's been hip to anything worth knowing about, and he's always been willing to pass that information on. He's the ultimate turner-oner. Yet when they read out the roll call of fêted music journalists – the canon of Kent, Bangs, Morley, Burchill, Shaar Murray et al – he never gets a sniff. Too jazz, probably. Too contrary, definitely.

At this point, I should declare a personal interest. I first met Brian when I was 16. He was a friend of my future wife's parents and he'd been told that I was into music. By that he automatically assumed jazz (what else is there?). Despite my protestations to the contrary, he followed me round the house simulating the hiss of Max Roach's hi-hat. Tsk, tsk, tsk!

I'd never met anyone like Brian. I still haven't. His knowledge and love for music flowed as swiftly and easily as the plentiful red wine he drank.

Occasionally, he'd pause on music and zigzag into books or films. He turned me on to some of the cornerstones of my life – Jim Thompson, *The Wild Bunch* and Gil Evans (the last of whom I named my first son after).

This book is an attempt to communicate something of that zeal as well as readdressing his co-ordinates in the critical universe. Its aim is to capture the unique and distinctive vernacular of one of the great – and overlooked – contemporary journalistic voices.

In a series of conversations conducted over several months, Brian offered vivid recollections of some of his most memorable encounters. As he did so, it became apparent that, added together, they formed a kind of parallel history of twentieth century culture. The result is this book, *On the Snap* – a thrilling encounter with a disappearing world, all delivered with the sharp, speedy insight of a great raconteur. We hope you dig it as much as everyone here at *Caught by the River* does.

Art Blakey

DRUMMER & BANDLEADER, 1919 – 1990

BLAKEY was very proselytizing. He was waiting for the big oil
crisis because it would cut off the electric instruments leaving just
the Jazz Messengers.

He said he learned how to drum from Chick Webb, who looked after
Ella Fitzgerald's early career. He was a little hunchbacked guy, she was
thin. I asked him what he'd learned and he said he'd learned how to roll.
He'd be asked to do it for ten minutes at a time until his wrists were
falling off. Webb had told him: 'You can always roll yourself out
of trouble in a number.'

A good story about Blakey is that one day he was driving through a
town in New England and there was a funeral. They had to slow down
because there were cars everywhere. They got out to hear the funeral
address and there wasn't much said. Art got up next to the priest and said,
very politely, 'If no one else has anything to say about the departed, can
I say a few words about jazz?' He never stopped selling. He was great.

I had a lot of sympathy with him. I loathed jazz rock and it was
always being fed to me by PRs. Fusion. Then it was smooth jazz. I hated
those Miles records. I thought they were rubbish. It wasn't what I wanted
from Miles. My collection ends with those Plugged Nickel records.
I couldn't see what all these wah wah trumpets were, electric pianos.
I could hear Weather Report were better than most but I didn't like them.
Life's too short for it. But Arturo's motto was 'opinions are like assholes.
Everybody's got one'.

Art Blakey

Art Pepper

SAXOPHONIST, 1925 - 1982

I WAS at Hull University and there was a kid who said he had a few
Art Pepper LPs. Not likely to hear about him from our librarian, that
prick Philip Larkin. I listened to them and thought, 'I've slept on this
cat. He's terrific.' I became quite obsessed by him. I got lots and lots of
his shit. His autobiography, *Straight Life*, that and *Raise Up Off Me* by
Hampton Hawes. They're the best jazz books.

When I interviewed him it was after he'd finished all his prison stuff.
It was much on his mind. Washing corpses, and the stuff they did to the
bodies, sexual stuff, was beyond belief. Then there were guys with big
dicks waving them around. It was like a sadistic homo situation. He hadn't
got much good to say for it. Lukewarm on TripAdvisor, man. I asked
him whether he saw any of his buddies in there and he had. Lots. Frank
Butler was one of his friends, a bad junkie but a great drummer. When
he was released Sonny Criss heard he was playing somewhere and he'd
come to hear him. Turned up with his dog. Art thought that was nice.
Art Pepper was very rambling. He was on methadone. He'd get fits of
trying to tie up even though he didn't need to do that any more. He'd cut
himself badly with wires. He was a fragile man to look after. He wasn't
what you'd call a solid citizen. He hated Chet Baker because he sang. Art
Pepper never gave up any names under pressure. Matter of pride to be a
stand-up cat. Everybody hated Chet because he informed.

Anyway, I saw him play in Hammersmith. Terrific. He played the way
all those late records sound. A bit too much Coltrane in there, led astray
a bit by that, but still very impassioned. Forcing it all in because of the
wasted years. He was very moved by the response. The audience went
off like a rocket when he walked on stage. Everybody stood up as if to
say, 'We know what you've been through and here you are. Good man!'
He then blew and played well after the time limit. Sensational! I went
backstage afterwards and he was very pleased that they'd liked it so much.

He was very eager to show that he still had a career and that he was working at it. I went to see Ronnie the night after and said, 'Why don't you book him?' Ronnie sucked his teeth and said, 'Art Pepper? You'll be saying Chet Baker next.' I told him he was clean, but Ronnie said he didn't know about that.

Another thing about his reputation as a junkie. I spoke to Dexter Gordon once and said, 'Christ, Art Pepper! Have you heard him? He's really playing.' Dexter said, real slow, 'With Art, playing wasn't the problem.' You can imagine how he said it, so much meaning under there.

Art and Laurie sent me a nice telegram after the piece came out.

Chet Baker

TRUMPETER, 1929 – 1988

I **CAN** remember that Chet was major despondent. A black cloud marking time. Why was I interviewing him? No particular reason. The Jazz Centre Society just asked me if I'd like to go on the road with him, and I said yes.

I wasn't crazy about Chet, in the same way that I wasn't really crazy about Miles. There's a certain sort of trumpeter who seems to exude a lot of self-pity – Chet did, sometimes Miles did. Aggressive, I preferred.

But I knew I was on to a winner in terms of writing about him. Actually, shortly after the piece came out, Derek Bailey grabbed me and said, 'I loved the thing you did on Chet.' Writing about fallen angels is schtick. It's a genre. I talked to Derek about that and he laughed. He was in flight from genre. It's such a well-trodden story, *Young Man With a Horn*, that book about Bix, all that stuff.

His music? I don't think he played badly. He was terribly professional. He never lost his love of playing properly and playing as well as he could. He'd sing melodies to me sitting on his bed. Twardzik's 'The Girl From Greenland'. He was still nuts about that music. The best image in the piece is me walking around some Midlands tank town in the rain looking for an Indian or somewhere to eat at 11 at night and I suddenly realized I'd lost Chet. He wasn't with me, he was about 100 yards back, camel coat with the belt lost and the cigarette burns, gazing in a pawn-shop window. I asked why he was looking, and he pointed to the trumpet and said, 'I was trying to see the name. You never know what a horn like that is gonna sound like.' That's great, isn't it?

The first time I ever heard him play I was in New York, not working for any paper, just a jazz nut. I looked in the *Village Voice* and there was a gig going on in a Strykers Bar. It was the Lee Konitz–Wilbur Little duo. I thought, 'That's for me. I'll go to that.' Anyway, it was terrific and then in the gloom, I heard this desolate trumpet and it sounded familiar. There was someone sitting right back on the stage amongst the stacked chairs. He had a Stetson on and cowboy boots. And it was Chet and he just played. He stayed in the shadows the whole time. You could see the light on the big African amethyst ring on his pinkie. 'Mister Chet,' breathed the bartender.

When I was on the road with him, Chet was travelling in a big people carrier and I joined him in that. The piano player was driving, I think. Chet didn't make much conversation, just sat there dumped. He looked like a skull. Every so often he'd say something mournful. Out of nowhere, he'd say, 'If I asked you, would you kill me?' You felt like saying, 'C'mon, Chet, pull yourself together!' I think he meant it though, he really did feel that bad. He was dreading doing an interview and kept eluding me.

At one point he cheered up. At least, I supposed he cheered up. A young Frenchman, in his early twenties, I guess, turned up and he and Chet retired to a private space. They'd obviously fixed and he was a bit more tractable at that time.

He spoke highly of things in the past – except Mulligan, they'd obviously quarrelled badly. He didn't want to speak about a lot of people because he'd shopped them, I suppose. He did talk about being picked to play with Bird. When Bird was on the west coast, he looked to audition a trumpet player to join him, and he chose Chet. That was before Mulligan, before Chet was known at all. There are records of him with Bird. At that stage he was similar to Miles, a little less hesitant, maybe.

I talk in the piece about putting him to bed and his dentures and all that stuff. His James Dean years had gone when co-eds had swooned clean out of their saddle oxfords, as someone memorably wrote. At the gigs, I could see middle-aged women who thought they could save him from himself. When I left him, he gave me an Austrian schilling and said, 'Have one on me,' like someone in a ghost story. When I heard he'd died, fallen out of the Amsterdam hotel window, on the nod, I suppose, I was very upset to hear it.

Al Pacino

ACTOR, B.1940

LIKE everyone else I was an Al Pacino fan. I thought he was a magic actor. *Dog Day Afternoon*, fantastic. *The Godfather*, fantastic. Anyway, I was offered a chance to interview him. I think it was for *Sea of Love*. Not a very good film, but it was nice to get the chance.

To juice myself up for this I had a video of *The Godfather* and I kept watching that scene when he's got to shoot Sterling Hayden in the café. He's never taken a human life before. He's not really of the Mafia, but he's got to do it. The others take him through it. How it's got to be: you have the meal, you ask to go to the toilet. They let you go to the toilet. You've got no gun, you go into the toilet and the gun will be strapped to the cistern. It's a noisy weapon, a .38 or something. We want a big bang so people run away. You come straight out and shoot.

Al goes into the toilet and there's this great scene with just him. You can see in his face his fear, it's written all over his boat race. He's twitching, staring, he's terrified. Anyway, he goes in and he kills them. I watched it until I knew every move of his face.

The interview was going to be at the Hyde Park Hotel at midday. That was in two days' or a day's time. I'd done all my homework and I came home and we'd been burgled. We lived in Brixton and they stole quite a lot of stuff, including the Colt 45 from my father who was a cop, CID in London. I wasn't going to kill anyone, but I knew it was illegal.

It came from a situation that wasn't illegal – my grandfather had it in Ireland as a cop. My dad never really used it. He fired it once in 1945 when the war ended. Another time he used it to shoot his income tax forms. He liked guns. I did too. Dad nailed his tax returns to a rowan tree and we stood back about 20 foot and blazed away. We shot them to bits. Anyway, I had the Colt 45 and a hundred rounds.

The rounds were what are called rimfire. If they're jostled together they go off. They're 1940s or something. Anyway, they'd stolen the .45, but they hadn't found the ammo. I wasn't keen on the fact that there was a gun out there, especially in Brixton, even if it was an antiquated weapon. I thought, 'Oh, Christ, we've got to have the police round. Don't anyone mention the gun.' I thought I better get the bullets out of the house. I took two polythene bags and I put fifty rounds in each. I put on my big trenchcoat and I put the bags in each of the side pockets. I was dragging that mackintosh around. I went off to *Time Out* and I thought I'll ditch these bullets *en route*. I'll throw them over the bridge into the water. The thing is, there are always people there. I passed a builder's skip and thought about putting them in there, but I thought if they're jostled they'll go off, so I couldn't leave them.

I walked through St James' Park, remembering the duck pond, but of course there's always people walking round the bloody pond. I arrived at the hotel. There'd been an IRA bomb scare and they were frisking people. This was where I had to go in to talk to Al Pacino. I had a rain hat on and I pushed the front up like Humphrey Bogart does in *The Big Sleep*, and pretended to be a tourist and walked in brandishing a map and went straight through security. Chutzpah!

I get in the lift and I get up to Al Pacino's floor and there's this big guy in front of his room, some kind of bodyguard. He didn't frisk me or anything, so I was sent into the room. I thought I mustn't take my mac

Al Pacino

off. I guess I thought the bullets would spill out of my pockets or something.

Al came in, all dressed in black, very short, as we know – totally nice, totally pleasant. He's whispering, 'Brian, why don't you take off your coat?' I said, 'I'll keep it on, Al, if that's OK.' He kept looking at my face. Christ, he's instinctive. My face was in the same state his face had been in when he played that scene. Twitchy man, twitch city. He kept asking, 'Are you sure you're OK, Brian?' Looking at me, trying to see my secret. I got through the interview. We went all the way round the houses, he never says much. It was OK, I got out of there. Fucking hell.

When I got home, the police had been round looking for dabs. I told my wife Sonia all about it. I said, 'We've got to chuck these in the Thames, but we've got to find the right bit.' We went to Greenwich, where there's a little park. There were three or four pensioners sitting on benches, it was early in the morning. By now, I'd put the bullets in two old paint cans. Full of pink or some shit colour. Sonia said, 'I'll create a diversion with the girls.' So she was dancing around, and I chucked them into the Thames. Thank fuck.

Days later, when I was transcribing the tape with Al, I finally found something to laugh at. We'd had a misunderstanding. He'd been talking about the armed services and I said that in the fifties I had been in the Mob. Al's eyes had grown wide with wonder. 'You were in the Mob?' I nodded. 'Why were you in the Mob?' 'I had to join,' I told him. 'Who said?' 'The government,' I replied. 'And I guess ultimately the Queen.'

Al seemed baffled.

The NME

MUSIC PAPER, 1952 –

THERE was a general impression among the rock writers when I arrived that jazz was something that went with pottery in St Ives, whereas I felt jazz was extremely alive and more exciting than the crap they were listening to. When I first started writing for them they were amazed, they realized they actually liked my style. I hoped that it would lead a lot of people into the music. Fat chance.

One person who was particularly welcoming was Charles Shaar Murray. He always wore these mirror shades. After a while I realized he was a completely self-regarding person, but I enjoyed that about him. As he moved around he was always checking himself out, making sure he was making a good shape. *Bella figura.* He was terribly witty and funny. He'd say, 'We made them a star last week, let's smash them this week.' He had an easy cynicism about him and I was amused by that. Charlie had the feeling that no gig could start until he was in his seat or at the bar, everything depended on him and that was it. He'd write at great speed and often you'd be about twenty lines into a piece before he mentioned what he was writing about it.

Nick Kent was also there at the time. He used to come in fairly irregularly, he didn't hang out at all. He used to take lots of small bits of paper out of his pockets and throw them down for the subs to piece together into some kind of story. He was always pretty wasted. His work never seemed finished, but it was full of lots of great phrases that he'd scribbled on the back of bus tickets. I liked the look of him. He looked like an El Greco wasted saint or something, like he should be peppered with arrows. He always had two pairs of leather trousers on – one covered the holes in the other.

Mick Farren was fairly truculent. When I first met him he was going out with a girl who was so pale she was virtually dead. I remember once, the whole office went on a treat down to the seaside somewhere,

Littlehampton, I think. We went to a place to eat, a pub, full of a lot of old people. They had a pool table in there. These old people all had piles of new potatoes and Mick – being high on, well, everything, I suppose – came in and started potting the new potatoes off their plates. It didn't go down very well. We had to leave.

The editor was Nick Logan, a pretty little mod. He knew he had an extremely volatile and talented crew so he didn't interfere too much. The deputy ed was quite different, we used to call him the Towering Inferno. Ex-Army, mad on Tolkien long before anyone else was, Tony Tyler. Tony was the ideas bloke, really. His manner was a bit like Boris Johnson's. He stuttered and, as he was trying to get the words out, he'd spin around going bright red. Everybody liked him. If you dropped copy round to his flat, he'd say, 'Watch out, that's so and so hill at the Battle of Waterloo at 3.10.' He'd have the whole thing laid out, little pink soldiers all over the carpet. He wasn't druggy. He was up there all the time anyway.

Suddenly, though, things changed. They were very slow off the mark with Johnny Rotten and all that lot. They thought the future lay in pub rock, bands like Dr Feelgood. They had no idea this punky thing was going to happen. Suddenly everyone started to cut their hair off and get a bit punkish, and they thought they should get some people a bit more in tune with this new rebellious, snot-gobbling thing. So they hired Tony Parsons and Julie Burchill. I left that same year.

Julie came on and she was about 16 or 17. She was totally mannered and you couldn't really understand what she was on about, and that awful little whiny voice. She didn't like being with the rest of the crew because some of them still had long hair. She got some maintenance people to build her a little office within the main office out of hardboard. Then she declared that she was a lesbian, so she tore out all these centrefold pictures and plastered the inside of her office with them. Everyone called the place Beaver Junction.

Parsons was all right. He got stuck with a feature on legal highs: senna pods, Sani-Flush. 'You're racing all right but you're throwing up.' The story goes that Mick Farren took Julie out on a date and they went back to his place. His sexual tastes were very, very odd. The next day Parsons weighed in and threatened to beat Farren up, so she saw him as her suedehead knight in shining armour. They married.

I loved being there, though. We'd all plant ourselves in the same pub and people would argue about each other's pieces. Everyone read everyone else's stuff. We'd argue and argue, drink and drink, laugh and laugh, it was great. Usually being a writer is a lonely thing, and being a jazz writer is even lonelier.

Don McCullin, Tim Page & George Rodger

WAR PHOTOGRAPHERS, B.1935, B.1944 & 1908 – 1995

I MET Don McCullin when he was working for *The Sunday Times*. I was freelancing at the time. I did Coppola for the cover of the mag. I was always in there touting for work and Don was always there too. It was about thirty-five years ago, about 1980.

Did I like his work? Not 'arf! I loved those war photojournalists. I knew him and I knew Tim Page, who'd lost part of his brain. I admired their courage, their composition under difficulty. I admired their guts and their work. What they did wasn't parcelled up for censors or anyone like that. It was in the moment, now's the time, like jazz. Don, of course, got banned from going to the Falklands. They didn't want that any more. Vietnam? It was terrible what they were doing there. Awful. I had the same politics that anyone left wing would have had.

The next time I met Don was when I was on some war film – [*Hamburger Hill*] and Don had done the stills for it. I interviewed the director, John Irvin, I think. I told him I wanted to talk to the stills guy. He was surprised.

Anyway, I went round to Don's gaffe then, a nice penthousey set-up. Neither of us were getting much work from *The Sunday Times*.

Evidently they just wanted him to photograph safari suits and they didn't want his stuff any more. The editor was that awful Scotch prannet who'd come in from Murdoch. Unconvincing syrup. We talked at length about the decline.

I asked him whether he was pleased with his stills and he told me that they were all right but you could tell that they were posed. He got very technical. He started explaining that these lights wouldn't have been there on a battlefield, things that I hadn't noticed. In a war the only light source would be the sun. He was good. He knew his stuff, obviously.

He talked a lot about being in war. He talked about how you were always thirsty. Fear. It's the fear that gets you. He got hit through the lens of his camera by a bullet. He talked about his eye being put out. I was talking about coming back from some music shindig and I told him I was wounded, as normal. 'You were wounded?' he enquired. 'From drink,' I explained. 'Oh, I really was wounded,' he said. Misunderstandings can get you a rich trawl. Er…sometimes…

We got on really well. His London background was a bit poorer than mine, fewer rooms, more in the bed, that type of thing. Mine was more lower-middle. We had quite a lot in common. We both came up around the time of the Teddy boys, we talked about that a lot. Every time he had a book out, I'd shoot round to Cape and we'd do an interview and go out and have a meal together. His London photos really spoke to me, especially his first newspaper break, 'The Guvnors', Teds in the bombed ruins. We were quite fond of each other.

He was always crisp. His older brother was army. There was a lot of army in Don. His clothes were sharp. I think he put it about a bit. I don't blame him with that life.

TIM Page? Well, I didn't like him very much. His house was in some little village in Kent. I asked him how I'd find it. He said, 'There's a row of cottages and there's one that's got hand grenades hanging outside.' It also had a load of signs in Vietnamese about the place. It wasn't shrunken skulls exactly but it was that kind of thing.

He was obviously a war veteran. He'd speak occasionally in Vietnamese French. He thought war was the greatest high in the world and he went on about it often – even though it had cost him part of his brain. His eyes wept continually. They took out something the size of an orange, apparently. He stood on a mine, shrapnel or something.

THE first one I ever did was George Rodger. He was the first photographer into Belsen and a founder member of Magnum. White haired, rather hawk-like face, an American wife, he was rather old when I met him. I did him somewhere down in Kent too.

He wore an English soft cap when he was at the front in the war and told me Patton passed through, pearl-handled guns, and shouted, 'Wear an American helmet.' Rodger told him he wasn't in his army. Patton said, 'I don't care. Wear an American helmet.' He said, 'I really can't. It hits the viewfinder.'

I asked him what it was like in Belsen. He said it was the turning point in his life. The dead, the dying, the skeleton-like people; he said he found himself arranging the dead bodies into a composition. At that point, he said he realized that he'd lost some part of his humanity. He wasn't high on war. He went to Africa afterwards. He stopped the war stuff. Wanted something more optimistic. He'd done all the Blitz and a lot of the Second World War. Good man, great photographer.

Duke Ellington

PIANIST, COMPOSER AND BANDLEADER, 1899 – 1974

ELLINGTON was doing a rehearsal for one of his sacred concerts in St Margaret's Church. He had all this music for the glory of God to be played in churches. I was freelancing for a paper called *Inside London*. It ran for three issues at a time when *Time Out* was on strike. It swarmed in and then it swarmed out.

I just went in and sat down on a pew right at the front. This was one time I was glad of my baggy eyes because he had them too. We both looked at each other and not a word was said. I probably didn't have the fun getting mine that he had getting his. Years later I interviewed Milt Jackson and asked him why his nickname was Bags. 'Why ain't yours?' he replied.

I thought Ellington was like a god. I don't know how he kept being so fertile and innovative and he'd been doing this shit since the '20s. He had incredible longevity and creativity, hardly ever rusted by routine. Very rarely.

Anyway, on this occasion, he had an English choir with him. Dreadful. Probably good for liturgical work, terrible for religious jazz. Ellington had this musical director with him called Roscoe [Gill Jr], and every time Ellington played a note, he would sing it and take it down to the choir who would flatten it. The choir was awful. No way down the alley. They were used to singing in a certain way without any inflection, certainly no black inflection. Duke decided to come back to it later.

What he had beside him on the piano was a coffee tin full of sharp pencils and lots of paper to write stuff on. Then he played something and it wasn't really that good and Ellington could feel that it wasn't quite fitting together and he shouted out, 'Harry, do your little thing here.' Well, Harry Carney had been with him for life, a baritone sax. He did something in there and it totally joined it up. He was a genius at stuff like that.

Duke Ellington

Just incidentally, Harry Carney used to drive Ellington when they went somewhere long distance. He was a good, reliable driver. And a drinker. Once they were stopped by the police. They didn't bother about Ellington because he wasn't driving. They got Carney out and Carney could hardly fucking stand. They told him to blow into the bag and he started doing that marvellous circular breathing that he could do. He was just blowing off the top of his lungs. The cops couldn't believe it, the machine showed up blank and they had to wave him on.

They rehearsed for about three hours or so, then came the cry, 'All press out. All press out.' I just stayed sat there and Ellington and me looked at each other with our baggy eyes and he didn't say anything. He didn't sell me out. I didn't write any notes in return. A lot of it was rehearsed but a lot of it was very ad hoc. He always knew that even if he couldn't pull something out of the bag, one of the great men in his band could.

Anyway, I wrote this piece up for the paper and I went round to deliver my copy, and there was only a cleaning woman in the office. I asked where they all were and she just said the mag had collapsed. Very shortly afterwards, the same year I think, Ellington died. I thought, 'Christ, I can hang this somewhere as a tribute.' I got on the blower and phoned a few papers and they weren't very interested. *Melody Maker* had a morgue on Ellington for decades. I phoned *NME* and they said, 'Oh, is he dead?' They asked how quick I could be and I told them that if they paid for a cab they'd got a piece right now. I shot round with the piece. They thought it was terrific and from there they asked me to be their jazz guy...

Gerry Mulligan

SAXONPHONIST & COMPOSER, 1927 - 1996

GERRY Mulligan was someone I'd idolized in my very earliest phase of loving jazz. The first jazz I'd ever heard was at a boys' club in Deptford that I used to go to. You'd play ping pong and billiards and try to pull the girls who sat on the radiators smelling funky. Unhygienic early fifties, man. Anyway, someone put on the Gerry Mulligan quartet – Mulligan and Chet [Baker]. I thought it was heaven. Shortly afterwards I saw a picture of Mulligan and he looked the way I wanted to look, which was tall, lanky, crew-cutted, gingery and Irish.

I idolized him as someone who blew this enormous baritone saxophone and didn't play it in a way that was barrelling or noisy or anything like that. He could play it slow. I thought that was wonderful. He loved to play with everybody. When he played with Getz, he was noodling around in the background, making Getz sound better. He was a really contributing player.

He also had all these marriages – one to Sandy Dennis this actress. She wasn't a film star, more a character actress. Then he had the big one to Judy Holliday. She was dying of cancer and Mulligan stayed all the time with her, like he was her carer. I thought that was good. Then I talked to Ronnie Scott about Mulligan and he said, 'He's an arsehole.'

Some musicians joke about what's the difference between a band leader and a bull. With the bull, the horns are at the front and the arsehole's behind. A lot of people said that about Mulligan, he could be a horrible bloke. He was bossy, wouldn't amend any of his ideas. He'd tell people off about their deficiencies, shout at people in public, all that. He was a perfectionist certainly.

He and Chet weren't best buddies. Mulligan got busted and went away. Chet wasn't caught and went on and made a nice quartet with Russ Freeman. When Mulligan came back, he offered Chet some money to rejoin the band and Chet didn't think it was enough. They didn't get along. Mulligan always took care of business despite the fact that he had a long heroin addiction. Chet didn't take care of business at all but became a romantic icon.

The time I interviewed Mulligan was in this not terribly ritzy hotel. I knocked on the door and I heard him say, 'Come in.' I went in and it was just a bedroom, it was tiny. His lady – it may have been his wife, someone Italian anyway – was in bed. There was a woman's bare back and half an arse sticking out of the bed. Gerry said, 'You better give the Countess five minutes to get ready.' So I waited outside and he got her into the bathroom.

He was very ready to answer questions, very matter of fact. He's a modernist but he's working the mainstream of jazz. He can play with Ben Webster, he can play with Johnny Hodges. He was always harking back and he could play piano well too.

There was period of time when he looked dreadful on his covers. He had a beard and long hippy hair. Terrible. I'd kept my crew cut. He was amused when I remembered liking that first bassist Joe Mondragon's wig best. 'But Joe was an Indian,' he said. Mulligan was all music, not fashion.

Gore Vidal

WRITER, 1925 – 2012

I WAS sent to interview him in Italy. He had a house in Ravello. It's up on a huge cliff, 1500 feet up then drops to the sea. I couldn't find out which one was his house because I was round the back of the villas and they didn't have numbers on them. I was out there for ages in the olive groves.

I finally pressed a bell and a voice – obviously Vidal's – said, 'What do you want?' I said that I was down to interview Vidal that day. He said that he was the butler and he'd see if Mr Vidal was in. It was him. He hadn't got a butler.

I told him I was glad to see a typewriter and he said he preferred not to use a computer due to the industrial military complex. He was full of theories about everything. He then showed me the view – 1500 feet down over a small railing. I looked and reared back. He loved that. He said, 'Ah, yes, Paul Newman had the very same reaction.'

Anyway, I interviewed him about *Billy the Kid*. Did I know that Governor Lew Wallace, who put a price on Billy's head, also wrote *Ben Hur*? I didn't. He started talking about how you could see *Billy the Kid* as Pan. He was talking about all this mythological stuff and lamenting that the film didn't deal with any of that. He thought Paul Newman was wrong for the part. No hooves. Before him, it had been Robert Taylor. All he'd say about him was, 'Oh my God, arthritic.'

He didn't have a good word to say about anyone much – except the Ancient Greeks and Romans. He thought the United States was going to hell in a handcart. He was probably right about that. He was a brilliant essayist. He signed all my books. He put: 'To Brian Case from Gore Vidal, 1500 feet about sea level.' He wanted me to always remember that I'd almost died from fear.

I left him after about an hour and a half and wandered off to find a café. Ravello is very small. There are about two cafés. I sat there having a coffee, full of relief at having got away. Cat could sneer for America. I looked up and I saw him shuffling across the square. He saw me there and said, 'Do you mind if I join you?' I said that was fine. He sat down and he was OK. He just talked Hollywood stories. He was outdoors and quite friendly. Finally I did get away!

Dexter Gordon

SAXONPHONIST, 1923 – 1990

I **SUPPOSE** like any jazz fan of my age, I fell in love with the first Blue Note records that came over here. In London, there was only one place where you could get them – Dobells on Charing Cross Road. I heard Dexter's 'Doin' Alright' and I was unaware that he'd had a career before Blue Note at that time. He'd been in prison for drugs, on and off throughout the '50s. Then he'd started to record for Blue Note and I heard him after the first two records when he came to Ronnie Scott's in 1962.

His sound was huge and so was he. He was 6' 5", very festive indeed, probably half-cut. He came on the stage and started to blow and stomp his enormous size-12 American brogues up and down seemingly in a different rhythm to the way he was playing. Great drops of sweat were falling off his head in slow motion. Sometimes he'd take the sax out of his mouth and start to sing. It was groovy, but it wasn't good singing. Anyway, Dexter stayed in my mind as one of my idols. You do have idols in jazz.

I finally got to meet him when I was writing about jazz. The Jazz Centre Society asked me whether I'd drive out to Heathrow and pick him up as it was all going to be too complicated for Dexter otherwise. I said I would. At that time I was driving a nearly broken down green Ford van. I drove out and parked and waited for Dexter.

There was no problem in spotting him. He was 6' 5", wearing the usual white trenchcoat and he had a saxophone case in one hand and a holdall in the other. Forgotten hotel keys, some on big wooden tags, hung from his pockets. I ran over and said, 'Mr Gordon, I'm your chauffeur.' He didn't say much. I hadn't realized he was probably quite shy. He followed me to the old green van and kind of smiled and got in. Off we went and it was raining like hell. I kept talking and he didn't say much. He wasn't hostile. He was probably just tired from the flight.

I got him to his hotel, a small narrow functional place somewhere off Holborn. I then arranged to come back the next day to do an interview. The next day, I hopped round to see him and he was taking stuff out of his bag. He took out a bottle of vodka and said, 'You might like a taste,' and he slid it across to me down the carpet.

I went and found a tooth glass, put my tape recorder down, and had a good slug at it. Because I was nervous, I did get through the whole bottle. I lay down on the very comfortable carpet and went to sleep and just before I passed out I heard laughter. I saw these giant size 12s step over me and walk out through the door. I was mortified with embarrassment. I phoned up later on and said, 'I'm so sorry.' He just laughed and laughed and laughed. He never stopped ribbing me after that. He always used to say, 'Could we do another of your interviews?' He was a gracious man with a huge sense of humour.

Anyway, once I phoned him up while I was in New York. He'd come back briefly from Denmark where he'd been living to stay away from the Man. He said that he had a gig to play to the prison population of Rikers Island Penitentiary and did I want to come. He'd done time there and he didn't feel very comfortable about being there without a friendly face. I said OK.

The van came for the prison, he went in a car with the guy who used to organize these prison concerts. He laughed when he saw me in the van. It had great hooks in it to manacle people to. When we got to the prison either the director was unaware that Dexter was an old alumnus or he tactfully didn't mention it, but he said, 'If we really like your playing, Mr Gordon, we'll keep you.' Dexter just growled.

There were guards with shotguns and about three hundred convicts. It was a hubbub of noise. Barons and cats with boob jobs. Anything that got you out of the cell was exciting, whatever it was. Dexter came on and announced all his numbers. '"The Panther" . . . "*El Pantero*".' That was for the Latinos. He blew his ass off for them. They screamed, '*Arriba! Arriba! Arriba!*' whatever he was playing. They just wanted to let off steam. I guess he knew it, because he kept going into a stomping thing.

Afterwards, they gave us a little lunch, which was awful. Grey prison bread. Dexter shaking his head. 'I got to eat this shit?' Then we were told we were getting out. I've never seen someone look more relieved.

Next time I was with him was on the set of Tavernier's *Round Midnight* where he was starring as a cross between Lester Young and Bud Powell. But he was sick and desperately tired, too tired to request one of my interviews. We talked about Lester and I told him how I dug his 'Clap Hands Here Comes Charlie' with Basie. Next day he delivered one of the highs of my life. He came in through the huge hanger doors of the studio, Lester's hat on plumb-line straight, blowing 'Clap Hands' right up to where I stood. I flipped, had to wipe my eyes.

Jack Nicholson

ACTOR, DIRECTOR, PRODUCER & WRITER, B.1937

I WAS quite scared before I met him. I knew he was intelligent and probably had no love of the press. I liked *Five Easy Pieces* very much. There was also a great scene in that terrible follow-up to *Chinatown*, *The Two Jakes*. He's a private eye and he comes into an office and sees this woman, Madeleine Stowe. He says to her, 'Kneel on the floor.' She kneels on the floor. 'Lift your skirt.' She lifts her skirt. She's got a plum-like behind. You could be up that like a rat up a rhododendron. He stands there by the water cooler, getting a glass of water, just looking at it. 'What an arse!' I said to him. 'You feel as I do,' he replied.

Anyway, I went in first. It was one of those things where they have six of you around a round table to do the interview. You all get the same shit and have to listen while all the other questions come in. Awful. Anyhow, when I went in, I thought, 'I'll be smoking and he smokes.' So I put my bag down on a seat and put an ashtray in front of it, and I knew he'd sit there next to me. There were a few ashtrays around. I picked them all up and hid them on a window sill.

He came in, saw the ashtray and sat just where I thought he would. The film was *Wolf* where he becomes a werewolf. It's not very good. Anyway, it seemed like there was a streak of light across his eyes. They seemed yellow. How? I thought, 'What the fuck's he doing?' He must have known the effect it would have.

One of the women interviewers had pinned a microphone on him and he took it off and he rolled up the wire until he got right up close and then wiggled his tongue at her. What a lecherous bugger! He answered the questions all right. He was good at that. I was more on his wavelength than the others. I didn't have any questions about knitwear. He talked about the alpha male in the wolf pack. He was interesting, very bright.

I'd heard somewhere that if you got Jack Nicholson on your film and there were things that needed fixing, he'd fix them. He was not just an actor. He said that that's how he'd always thought it should be, actors should contribute, they should be in the boiler room. If he could make something better then he would. He did direct a couple of things. I thought he was red hot. He sampled my rollups.

I caught him in the lobby afterwards drinking a pint of orange juice or something. He was like Ginsberg in his final years, he dressed horribly. Blazers. He had very short legs. He once said, 'They're short but they work.'

Ian Dury

SINGER, 1942 – 2000

THE paper [*NME*] thought I should do Dury, so I read the words on that *New Boots and Panties* record and thought they were terrific. His writing is just so funny.

We got on. A lot of my friends were art school. I was ten years older than him but our reference points were very much the same. We both idolized certain black and white film stars – Alan Ladd, for instance. Ian loved him because of the height thing. If I mentioned a record, he was on it. Books, the same. He knew everything. He was a knowledge box. A good painter too. Not that you'd want one, but they're really good.

He knew a lot about jazz and liked a lot of it. He had interesting views on the cultural scene. He may have had other areas he knew that he didn't talk about with me. My knowledge is limited but in that area we saw eye to eye on a lot of things.

We both loved rhyming slang. Ian always had ones that I'd never heard. If I had one, I'd tell him and he'd laugh. A stall holder once said to me, 'Don't you want your rifle?' I didn't know what he meant. 'Rifle?' 'Rifle range, your change. Cunt!' Ian loved that.

Once we walked past someone selling cucumbers and heard the guy say, 'This way for your Piccadilly comforters!' It didn't really work but it was funny. We both decried the fact that all those TV shows like *Minder* had introduced made-up ones. They were a bit Sexton. Sexton Blake, fake.

I knew of his terrible moods but I never experienced them. He could by all accounts be vicious in all directions. I would have made allowances but I never ran into any. I saw members of his band in tears sometimes. He would lash out all right.

Although he liked American culture, he didn't like Americans very much. He thought they were overfed swine. Edward G. Robinson bought one of his paintings while he was at art school. He was a collector. Ian was a very English icon, really. Music hall. We'd laugh at some of those old acts. The White-Eyed Kaffir was one. Obviously you couldn't get away with being called that now if you were a white man. Ridiculous.

We knew people who were common to the art-school scene. He knew Peter Blake, though, and I didn't. Peter would turn up to some of the gigs, sit quietly in the wings and draw Ian, or whatever. I pretended I didn't know his pedigree . He had a few rejects on the floor. I picked one up and said, 'Not bad, not bad. I'll keep that one if you like.' Ian came over and said, 'You fucking cunt, you know who he is, don't you?' Nice try.

Once, we were in San Francisco and there was a radio station just outside that was doing an interview with him. They laid on some kind of drinkie-poos for us all. One of them slipped me something, an animal tranquillizer of some sort. They put it in my drink. I didn't know. I wandered out of the reception and went and sat outside. Oh God. It was terrifying to me. I never did LSD. I couldn't find myself and my teeth seemed to be eating each other. In the end, Ian came out and saw me sitting there, totally mad, so they got me in the band bus, where I started thrashing about. They tied my arms down. Eventually they got me back to the hotel and strapped me to a bed. I lay there chewing my cheeks until the next morning. Years later, I saw Ian just before he died and he said, 'We thought we'd lost you there. Man overboard!'

I missed him when he died. I was very sorry. I went to the wake afterwards. I knew how ill he was. He took me to his house and showed me the machine he was on. He was on it every day, nine hours a day, changing his blood. He had this spout set in his belly. Too risky, as he used to say. He had great courage. He said to me, 'I've always been ill.' And he had been. He was in a lot of pain but he just got on with it. To our cockney Valhalla.

James Ellroy

WRITER, B.1948

I FIRST came across him when I read *The Black Dahlia*. I went to interview him – he was going to a thriller writers' festival in the French Alps. A train had been put on by the sponsors, some kind of brandy and some kind of champagne. That stuff was all free and we had about six hours on the train. The train was packed with thriller writers. I found Ellroy easily enough. He was massively tall, with the glasses and everything.

James Ellroy

I introduced myself and said could we talk. He said, 'YES! YES!' He was like a junkie, his leg tapping all the time. I said, 'Let me tell you a story first.' My father had been a cop and I told him about a time he'd been on a stakeout at a warehouse in Whitechapel, some place like that. He'd been there all night. They'd had a squeak that it was going to be turned over, but nothing.

Suddenly, in the early morning, my dad heard this awful groaning noise. He went to investigate and found a bloke in the corner dying. He'd cut his throat but there was no weapon. Dad went and found a phone box and got the squad in. He thought it must be murder. Then they did the autopsy on him. He was obviously a neat cat because he'd cut his throat and dropped the razor down his windpipe. It was inside him. I told James this and he virtually screamed, 'YES! YES! YES! YES! Can I use it? Can I use it?'

Another time I was talking to him and he said he was going to use Art Pepper in a book. And I said, 'You know he was a junkie?' And he said, 'No.' Didn't know he was a fucking junkie? How the hell can you not know that?

He had a grotesque turn to his mind. I have some of it too – probably inherited from my dad and the war and all that. He was obsessed with a serial killer in LA. He used to gouge out women's eyes and then jack off into the sockets. He was called the Night Stalker. James loved things like that, absolutely loved them. He makes big statements. Some of them are racist. He was a motormouth. Someone asked him about the Korean population of LA. He just shouted out, 'They eat dogs!' He was like that.

He spied on women when he was younger. He'd look in on them dressing and undressing. He was pulling himself off all the time. I spoke to his publisher once, Otto Penzler, and he said he went to Ellroy's first marriage and as the bride was at the altar Ellroy came crawling up the aisle, pulling himself by the hair and barking like a dog. He said, 'He is crazy. Totally crazy. He loves Hitler and all that Nazi stuff. He's maybe a Nazi. He likes the ceremonial of it all. It impresses him. Wagner, Beethoven, rallies, he likes all that. I don't know how political this all gets, but he's obviously way off to the right of the Republican Party. We know that.'

I watched him at a book signing once. Someone asked him to sign to Dick. 'Dick? Is that Donkey Dick?' Ellroy bellowed. In my copy of *The Big Nowhere* he wrote, 'White jazz slashes throats!'

Jimmy Smith

ORGANIST, 1925 - 2005

MAX Jones, who was the guru on *Melody Maker* – he really did know about jazz, he lived the life almost – told me once that when I went to interview black American jazz musicians I should always take a bottle of brandy with me. So I did.

When I met Jimmy Smith, he was in a furious temper in Hammersmith. They'd damaged some valve in his Hammond and he didn't know if they'd be able to repair it or if he'd have to avoid some keys. He was livid. I said, 'You probably need a taste, Jimmy.' He did.

He was the most bombastic man you could possibly imagine. Even more so than Illinois Jacquet. He invented everything. Everything was him. I asked him about Larry Young. 'Tall feller, learned everything from me.' He may have done initially but he definitely diverged into his own thing.

I loved the suits he wore on his early Blue Note covers – shiny, mohair, beautiful suits. 'Yeah, the bitch took them,' he said. He'd obviously lost them in divorces. He was a real pussy hound.

The best thing he said is in the piece. He was in a warehouse with his organ trying to master it, and when he was ready he came out 'like a stallion'. He did too. Those early records are killing. He could really do it.

The reason why you don't see a lot of interviews with Jimmy Smith is because he swore all the time – 'motherfucker, motherfucker, motherfucker' all the time. And no one was any good apart from him, so you had to do a certain amount of pruning to get any sort of story at all.

Thurber wrote a short story once about a bloke who was an aviator.

Jimmy Smith

He's the first person to cross the Atlantic, in the story. The president wants to send him on a tour to show American pluck, but as soon as he speaks it's all f-this, c-that and the president gives a nod to one of his aides, who pushes him out of the window. A safe dead hero. He's not saleable. Jimmy Smith was a bit like that.

The first time I saw him was at a concert where I was just a punter. I was surprised to see so many blacks in the audience. You didn't get that much in jazz. They were all wearing stingy-brimmed hats and as soon as Jimmy started playing 'Back At The Chicken Shack' they all threw their hats in the air. I don't know how they ever got the right ones back. That really is flipping your lid! So good!!

Johnny Griffin

SAXOPHONIST, 1928 - 2008

HE was fast. Fast! It was at a time when critics thought it was useless to be fast. What's that all about? Fast? Fast! But he thought that fast. His mind was fast. In fact, his metabolism might have been quite extraordinary. He'd be talking to you nineteen to the dozen and then he'd suddenly fall asleep in mid-sentence. Like that, instant. He wasn't a drugger. He'd left America to get away from that scene. He was just an alcoholic.

How did I get into him? I read a review in *Jazz Monthly*, which was a really good mag, by Jack Cooke. Jack said his record was only twenty-eight minutes long. Christ! And it cost over thirty shillings! Anyway, he raved about it and I thought I just had to check it out. I was at Hull University at the time and the chances of seeing a Blue Note up there were nil, so I hitchhiked down, went to Dobells and they had a copy.

It had a cover picture by Andy Warhol, which meant nothing to any of us. I thought it was crap. I wanted a picture of Johnny Griffin. Blue Notes always had great photos. Why did I want this fucker? I listened to it, *The Congregation* was the name of it, and just thought, 'Christ, that's great!' It just hooked me. After that, as they came out, I bought his records. I don't think I missed any.

Then he was due to come to England and he was due to play at the Bull's Head in Barnes. I don't know what that was all about. Quite a few people would turn up there. Ben Webster would be there regularly. Anyway, Johnny came on. He was very small, about 5' 1" or something. And of course the sight of a tenor in the hands of a small man makes it look like an enormous horn.

And he played, eighty, ninety bars a minute. Re-entry goggles all round. He was no good on ballads unless he could up 'em. I can't remember who the drummer was but he was tiring after a minute. Johnny was convivial, shouting and yelling and enjoying. When he wasn't playing, he always clapped in triplets – clap, clap, clap – to urge the rhythm section on.

It turned out Tubby Hayes was in the audience. Tubby got up, went over to him and said, 'Do you mind if I sit in?' Johnny had mocking eyes, real jive-ass motherfucker eyes, and he looked at Tubby and just said, 'If you think you can.' He wasn't being funny. He knew he was fast and didn't know who Tubby was. Tubby was fast though and Johnny loved it and then they chased each other – on and on and on. It became a duo. It was just heaven. 'Yeah, Fatty!' Well, he got that wrong. He and Tubby became hellraising buddies in the Clarke–Boland Big Band. 'We were thrown out of all the nice towns in Switzerland – taken right to the train station.'

When I interviewed him years later, I was struck by just what a rapid speaker he was. His moods changed very, very quickly. You could see that he could be quite a dangerous guy. It was the way he played. One critic said that Johnny's playing sounded like he wanted to fight all the time. That was true but it made my soul want to fight along.

I'd always go and see him at Ronnie's and I went to see him in New York at some raggedy old festival. I saw him and said, 'Johnny!' He just walked past as if I hadn't spoken. Then he came back and said, 'Damn, I shit on a face!' He had a group with Eddie Lockjaw Davis, and Davis was a pretty stately piece of work, a lovely fella. You can see on some of the covers that Griffin has just cracked a joke and Davis is laughing and Griffin is looking like he hadn't said anything. He was a jive-ass motherfucker verbally. I loved that about him.

Michael Caine

ACTOR, B.1933

I HADN'T really cared about all that swinging London stuff and, of course, he'd been in all that. Then I saw the one set in Newcastle – *Get Carter* – and I thought, 'Fuck, he's good. Menacing and good.' I'd seen him over the years in various films and I guess I'd got used to him, his voice, his mannerisms, he was a known quantity.

I'd watched him to try to get an Oscar in *The Quiet American*. He was all right. He cried in it and wimped in it, squeezed the old curtains. Of course, he was extremely annoyed when he didn't win.

People who'd done him before said to me that he was totally uncooperative. I went in and stressed the Cockney a bit more, threw in a few rhyming slangeries and he took to me. We'd lived not far from each other in London. I asked him whether he'd been a Teddy boy, and he said that he'd only half been. 'You could get duffed up if you dressed like that.' He's about two or three years older than me. He's tall as well – about two or three inches bigger than me.

He will lie, which I don't mind. I asked him how he lost all the weight he put on for *Shirley Valentine*. He said that he'd spent hours on the rowing machine, the cycling machine, running, dieting. He'd put the hours in. Later on someone else told me he hadn't done any of that, he'd just had liposuction. That's much more like Caine. On liars, when I first went to interview him, the taxi driver told me he'd known Caine when he was Maurice Micklewhite. Childhood mates, they'd climb through the fencing around the blitzed theatre at the Elephant and play inside. They'd raise and lower flats, dress as pirates and sword-fence from the opera boxes. 'That's where he got the idea of being an actor,' said the cabbie. I told Caine. He laughed. 'Bollocks. I was evacuated to the country with my mum.'

He'd done so many films but he was still insecure, the way actors are, thinking it will all go away. He said that when he was picking what film to do, he liked to see where it was set. If it was set somewhere sunny and it was February in London, he'd do it. The weather. One time I interviewed him in Ireland and there was a tiny bit of sun and he came straight out of his caravan to soak up this tiny little patch of warmth.

We talked about all the early stuff. They weren't even b-films, they were fillers made for tax purposes. Caine was in a couple of them. I asked him how he got into them. He said he hadn't been on the screen before but he looked tall so, at an audition, someone said he could be a copper. They then gave him the copper's uniform, but it absolutely stunk from being worn by nervous young actors. They'd never had it cleaned. Caine's quite a fastidious man so he took it to the cleaners. Had it totally cleaned. Cost all his wages. He didn't have any lines in the film, he just stood around in this spotless uniform, and he said the bloke who was auditioning these tall young hopefuls was cross-eyed, so he'd say, 'Right, you.' And everyone would jump up because no one could tell where he was looking. He was very funny on his early days.

He'd never learned to drive, so all those films with him driving are a lie. He wasn't particularly salacious. I don't think he was on the prod. Maybe when he was younger, when he was sharing a flat with Julie Christie and Terence Stamp. I think that's it, really.

Norman Mailer

WRITER, 1923 - 2007

I ALWAYS enjoyed his books. Not all, some are awful. *Why Are We In Vietnam?* – awful. When he was on song he was great. *The Armies Of The Night*, fantastic book. *The Executioner's Song*, fantastic. Untouchably

Norman Mailer

good. He was pugilistic, aggressive, all that stuff. By the time I met him he was getting on a bit.

The first time I got him I wasn't down on the list of people who were due to interview him. I just popped my head round the door after the last one had gone and said, 'I'm not on your list, Mr Mailer, but I'd like to ask you a few things.' He told me to come in. He was friendly.

I'd just gone through a divorce and I said that he'd written in one of his books about marriage, that 'to stay in the same place, the ante goes up.' He said that you learn that. 'Fucking right,' I said. So we talked about that and he was good, very honest.

I told him how much I liked American literature. It was all I read, really. He just said that in a way it was all over. He thought his generation, him and Roth and people like that, were like the second XI compared with Hemingway, Fitzgerald, Faulkner. That was the real team, and you couldn't put one together that good now. He thought the times had changed, people weren't looking at novels much any more. They were into TV, or whatever. He talked a lot about all that stuff.

When he was younger he was very feisty, punching people and all that, but he wasn't like that at all on the occasions when I met him. He was small, bow-legged. I liked him very much. He was courteous as hell and he'd really explain things to you.

He wrote a book about the particular period when the CIA was being run by James Jesus Angleton, who was technically insane. Getting them to tunnel under Berlin to get into the Russian zone. Mailer's book was meant to be in two parts, but he never bothered with the second part. The first part was about a thousand pages.

Anyway, he explained all about it – as if I hadn't read it or at least hadn't retained much of it. He was very keen to help you understand. He made for very good copy, often very thought provoking. I know other American writers have said that he was jealous of their success. DeLillo didn't like Mailer at all. When he was doing his Oswald book [*Libra*], Mailer had been very discouraging. He didn't always present nicely and politely, but he did to me. Maybe because I'd started off with the ante going up...

Richard Harris

ACTOR, 1930 – 2002

I **WAS** very fond of Richard Harris. I'd fallen for him in *This Sporting Life*. We'd not had a hero like him before, one who looked like he could punch your head in. He was a big muscular guy, and Irish as well. He was like my dad. Lindsay Anderson loved him.

I saw him at the Royal Court. This was centuries ago. A Gogol play, I think – Russian anyway. He was good. He's an animal on stage. Whether he was a good actor or not I couldn't say, but his presence was incredible – all the prowling menace. I then saw him again. I can't remember what it was, *Henry IV* or something.

Anyway, next day I interviewed him in Guildford. I got there and he was still in his pyjamas. He immediately ordered us two enormous grease-ups. There were eggs and bacon and sausages and fried tomatoes, mounds of the stuff. It all arrived and he started asking me, 'What did you think of me in the play? What did you think?' Total ego. I said, 'Well, there's a lot of coming and going at the start before you come on. I'd cut that down.' He picked up the phone and immediately called the director and told him what I'd said. He even tried to get me to speak to him. It just had to be all about him. I could see what he was like. Jesus!

And he was getting through directors at the rate of knots.

He lived some of the time in the West Indies. He'd bought a house out there when he was a star. He lived there quite a lot. He said, 'I've got a few of the proper lads from the old sod over there with me.' His house was on a very small island, and one day the British under-consul said he was going to come and visit. When it was time for him to arrive, Harris put some porn on the television and told his friends to get their dicks out and then he went and answered the door and brought this guy in. That was his idea of a joke.

That was when he was drinking. I asked him when he'd stopped, and he said, ' 'Eighty-seven, 1 April, at 10 p.m.' I asked him if he regretted it, and he said that not a day went by when he didn't. For his last drink, he'd ordered two bottles of Château Margaux, 1943, very expensive. He'd just sat there and drank the lot. He'd decided it was the last liquor he'd ever have. Then he did the vow – although I bet he could hardly walk by then.

He was very friendly with O'Toole. He'd always say, 'O'Toole's very sly. Very sly!' He told me about a time when they were both at a club trying to pull the same woman. They both invited her for a drink and they went somewhere in Maida Vale. They went to one of their flats, on the fifth or six floors. He said, 'I was just about to go in there with her but O'Toole slipped past me, pulled the girl with him and slammed the door. I was locked outside caterwauling like an old tomcat. I wasn't going to have that.'

Anyway, he rang and rang and there was no answer, so he went outside and saw a light on, realized that was the flat they were in and got hold of the drainpipe and started to climb it. He got up to a point where it started coming away from the wall. O'Toole came out on to the balcony with his arm around the girl and said, 'Goodbye, Richard.' Then the police turned up and he spent all night long in the cells. 'Fucking O'Toole. That's what he did for me.' He had some great stories, he was full of stuff like that. On stage in Shakespeare he'd got the cast to hold their hands up cupped for the line, 'This gives us pause.'

Later, I'd been on a set with him up in the Arctic. It was for *Miss Smilla's Feeling for Snow*. It was in the north of Sweden, up near the nuclear sites up there. Kiruna. It was all snow and howling wolves – an awful place. It was where Swedish children were told Santa Claus comes from, but he doesn't. He comes from Deptford. He gave Christopher Marlowe something he didn't want.

There's a copper mine there and they've dug up a small mountain and flattened off the top and put sodium lamps all over it. The local people work there. A lot of them are Laps. They're drunk all the time and you see them all over the place lying in vomit on the snow. There are oil drums that have cracked open and are rusting. They're lying around all over the place. Anyway, I was there with Harris. He had a Guinness. 'Just one, it's medicinal. Purely medicinal.'

He did a sensational thing on that shoot. He had to die by falling into the Arctic seas. He had a rubber suit on with belts so they could hoick him out quick, because you'd die pretty quickly in those freezing waters. Harris had to put this black suit on. He hated it. 'It's like being in a condom,' he said. He hurled himself in bravely. There are shots of him in the film clinging hold to an iceberg. He was freezing to death, but he did it. Then he phoned all his ex-wives to tell them how brave he'd been.

Roland Kirk & Ornette Coleman

SAXONPHONIST, 1935 – 1977, & SAXOPHONIST & TRUMPETER, B.1930

I SAW Rahsaan at Ronnie's at various shows. He was wonderful at getting the crowd going. Once, he had a big sack of little penny whistles with him, and we had to blow them during 'Here Comes The Whistleman'. That was a lot of fun. He was fun to watch.

I interviewed him after he'd had a stroke. I was interested to see what he'd done with the horns. He had all sorts of pickling-jar elastic bands going from this key to another horn. Now that one of his arms didn't work very well, he'd worked out a system where he could still play three horns at once with one arm. Outa sight! They'd told him in the hospital after his stroke that he mustn't do anything strenuous again and that he must never play music again. I said, 'But you are.' And he said, 'Hospitals don't know shit about the saxophone!'

He was with one of his grandchildren and he was stroking its hair very lovingly while he was doing the interview. He was very tactile. Blind, of course. He talked about circular breathing and why he wanted to do it. He said that's how you know you're alive, the continual hum of the sun on your head, and he wanted the continual hum of breath in his body.

Ornette went on about things like that, being mystical. When I asked Ornette about *Skies Of America* he said that growing up in Fort Worth, Texas, racism was terrible. He said you never knew where you were with whites – some would smile at you, some would try to kill you. It was like weather. You didn't know whether it was going to piss down on you or be sunny. He said there were places he'd lived where one side of the road there'd be hailstones and on the other side of the street it would be sunny. He felt white people were like that to him.

Ronnie Scott

SAXOPHONIST & CLUB OWNER, 1927 - 1996

I USED to go up the West End when I was in my teens, keen on jazz. I probably went to more clubs in New Cross, which was near where I lived. I think the first club I went to was Club 51, in one of those little side streets off St Martin's Lane. I could hear music coming up from the basement and, a bit like in that film *'Round Midnight*, I was outside listening in. It was probably Tommy Whittle or somebody like that. I thought that was great.

The first time I went to Ronnie's it was 7 shillings and 6 pence to get in. Bloody hell, they're coming it! It was the Old Place. The first place I heard Dexter Gordon. Bloody hell, that was worth 7 and 6. Dex was drunk and I was smack up against the bandstand, on the level with his enormous shoes. They were stomping slowly, about half the time of the rhythm he wanted. It meant something to him. He was singing a lot. He liked to do that, especially if he'd had a drink or two. He was blowing... Jesus, it was wonderful. It was '61. I thought, 'This is the place to be.'

What was it like in there? General feeling of Soho, all the bohemian characters were there, a lot of musicians hanging out and talking. It was pretty downmarket in terms of what you could get and where you sat. It was very rickety, very hot, like a cavern. It had good people. That was what drew you, it wasn't the amenities. It was full of smoke, of course, smoke everywhere. Zoot came in. He could swing you into good health!

How did I get to know Ronnie? I think it was while I was at the *Melody Maker*. He was scary. He knew me then because there was always someone from *Melody Maker* to review the opening night of whatever run was on. It meant that he told the bar I drank for nothing. I talked to him a bit and tried to tell him jokes that never went down terribly well. I thought they were bloody funny. He'd either heard them or he was the man with the jokes. It was one or the other.

I knew the door very well – Roxy Beaujolais. Liked her. She had brassy, dyed ginger hair, big *poitrine*. She had a television cooking show recently. She runs a pub somewhere. She's Australian, she's Jewish, but you're not to know that because she's Roxy Beaujolais not Jenny Hoffman. She didn't have my respect for Ronnie, probably because he was a womanizer, and because she's a Jew she sees through the schmatter.

Then there was Fat Henry Cohen. Do you remember Fat Henry? He was about 20 stone. He was like one of those fat Mafia hard men you see round Frank Sinatra. I wouldn't call him 'Fatty'. He was rolling a joint with one hand. Someone would be making a noise in the club and the call would go out: 'Fat!' He went in and he didn't hurt whoever it was. He'd wear them out. They'd punch him until they were worn out. I remember once, as he was chucking someone out, he said, 'If you fucking come back, I'll set fire to your moustache.' I'd take Robert Wyatt down there. I was driving a van. We'd get the wheelchair all set up and Fat Henry would say, 'I like it when you come. It makes a change chucking someone into the club!'

Anyway, Ronnie... Did I tell you the thing he said about Joe Pass? Joe had just stumbled off a plane from the US and had come straight to the club and played a rather curtailed first set, less than half an hour. He was worn out. He wanted to have a cup of coffee or something. As he was leaving the stage, Joe Pass said, 'I guess that will take care of that.' Ronnie shouted down the microphone, 'Guess again!' And poor old Joe had to go back and play a couple more. Once, *Melody Maker* was late with its tribute to the club's anniversary, and when I went into his office as usual – he just lifted up one bum cheek and farted loudly. My review. Ronnie could be rough. He had to be. There were gangsters in there, right back to when all those Maltese gangs were running all over the place. He was used to dealing with lowlife. Ronnie loved musicians and he loved actors.

It was very East End. If they accepted you, and you were a stand-up geezer, you were in. And I was, I went three times a week, never missed a gig, never gave an unfair review. Ronnie once said about a review, 'It wasn't as good as you said, Brian.' I told him it worked for me, and he said, 'It worked for you. You can't read fucking music, can you?' He was always frank. They called me family and it felt good. This was my world and I was in it.

Sam Fuller

SCREEN WRITER AND FILM DIRECTOR, 1912 - 1997

I INTERVIEWED Sam Fuller when *White Dog* came out. Did you see that? The racist dog. It's not terribly good. It's one of his really bold assumptions. In this case, that you can train a dog to attack a black man. It's about reconditioning them. He talked about that.

I was doing him for *The Times*. He sat there with a huge cigar. When he knew who I was writing for he said that he was a newspaper man. He went on and on about that. He also talked about the books he'd written.

He'd done one called *The Dark Page*. It's about the editor of a newspaper who sees that there's not much going on. It's a dull read, so he thinks he'll ginger it up, and he goes out and serial kills, getting a few scoops for his reporters along the way. I said that I'd like to get hold of that and, soon enough, through the mail from Paris where he lived, this book duly turned up. Inside he'd written – as if I was Winston Churchill or something – 'To Brian Case, Whose blood, sweat and tears are part of this 1949 book.' Fantastic. I've still got it. He was extremely likeable. I just couldn't get him on to his films.

He just wanted to talk about papers he'd been on, legendary newspaper men he'd known, all of that. He gave me about an hour and

Sam Fuller

half on all that. He'd discovered the body of Jeanne Eagels. There was
a film made about her. When he found her there was a bit of torn-off
brown paper and written on it was something like, 'I can't take no more.
I'm so sorry to everyone. Goodbye.' Something heartbreaking like that.
He'd remembered it.

He said his mother wouldn't let him eat with them. She said he smelled
of formaldehyde. He probably did, he spent so much time in morgues
and stuff. He'd been in the '20s riots in Harlem. He'd seen how the cops
behaved. He was totally pro-black. You'd think he was an anarchist from
his films. There's no one good in them. Actually, he was like a real old
Democrat. He was small, bandy, likeable. He was similar in that respect to
Mailer. He was a certain American type.

He was a crime reporter. He'd seen nothing but violence, bad
behaviour, greed, death. He was nothing like Ellroy. Ellroy took a
delight in it – as bad as possible. Fuller wasn't like that at all. He was
matter-of-fact.

Eventually we got on to Rod Steiger in the *Run of the Arrow*. Fuller
hadn't cared for him at all. He thought he was a coward – even though
Steiger had been in the navy. It was all because when Fuller started a film
he'd fire his Colt 45 in the air. When he first did it, Steiger hurled himself
on to the ground. Quite sensible, really. As far as Fuller was concerned
though, that meant he was no good. The man was a wimp. He was a
Caspar Milquetoast, as the Americans say.

When I interviewed Steiger, I brought this up. He said, 'Fuller, he
almost gave me a bloody heart attack. He fired a .45 right by my ear. The
man's a maniac.' They'd gone off each other in a big way.

Fuller also had no time for James Dean. He thought it was wimpy,
snivelling. He didn't think they should show that. He liked Lee Marvin.
He would!

In the context of the time, his films were staggering. I saw the first
one when I was quite young. I'd never seen violence like it. It was *Pickup
on South Street* with Richard Widmark, who's a pickpocket. There's a
great performance in there by Thelma Ritter, who plays a fence.
At the end, Widmark gets hold of one of the bad guys and he drags

him across the railroad tracks and you see his head go bump, bump, bump and you think, 'Christ, how did they do that?' It was really violent. I thought, 'This is for me.' I loved it. His films stuck out for their violence and for their weirdness. From that point on, whenever he had a new film out I'd go and see it, and he never let me down. He was even more extreme than Hitchcock. He once said he'd like it if real guns could be fired over the heads of the audience as they were watching.

He never really realized he was an artist, which was good because he never got pretentious. I loved him.

Sex Pistols

PUNK GROUP, 1975 - 1978

THE *Observer* wanted someone who had no feelings one way or the other about punk. The press was full of stuff about it, people being gobbed on and pogo'ed at. A flying glass had cut someone's face at that 100 Club show. There was an anti-punk thing happening, like there had been with Teddy boys, I suppose. They wanted someone who had no interest in it at all. I didn't know who the fuck they were. I thought a punk was someone in prison who got fucked up the arse. Anyway, I agreed to do it.

They obviously thought it was going to be a rough house so they said that they'd give me Big Don, a large photographer. So I had to meet him in some pub on Fleet Street. I asked how I'd know him, and they said, 'Well, he's 6' 6" and wears a maroon suit. You'll figure it out.' I met him and he was one of those big guys that you know you could put on the floor if you wanted to. Anyway, he had a terrific car and he drove us up to where they were. That wasn't easy to work out because their gigs were blowing out at a rate of knots. This was after the whole 'fuck-off' thing on the Bill Grundy show on TV. They had three gigs left out of fifteen, something like that, anyway.

We got one somewhere in Wales, Caerphilly, I think. Their gig there had got cancelled but a local entrepreneur had said they could use his fleapit cinema, so they did it there. Outside, there was a protest organized by the local vicar. 'Don't let the antichrist come to your town!' All that. 'Don't go in there, you'll get contaminated,' he said to me. I told him I was a journalist and he said, 'Oh well, you're already contaminated anyway.' So I went in and I met them. They were totally hostile, professionally hostile.

I said to one of them, '[something], man.' And then they just bleated back, 'Maaaaaan, maaaaaan.' I just thought, 'You cunts.' Anyway, I tried to talk to them. I can't remember anything Rotten said, but he must have spoken. I just remember he had green all over his teeth. He had fucking awful teeth. The only interview that did land on me significantly was the one with the manager, Malcolm McLaren. He may even have had that woman who became the fashionista with him, Vivienne Westwood. He was a hustler of the highest order in a fluffy pink jumper. You admire it. There was me trying to talk to him, the *South Wales Argus* and some other paper, and he fielded us all in the tone that we'd need for our piece. Boom, boom, boom. Then he'd intertwine – he was fantastic. I thought he should be the star here. He was terrific.

Then the band did their stuff: Rotten, knees chained together, gobbing. He just reminded me of Pinkie in *Brighton Rock* – little and nasty. The audience – very few got through the Watch Committee, there were only about fifteen of them – were huddled together. It was freezing out but they all had suspenders and bare thighs. They were flying the flag for what they believed in, I suppose. I liked them. I asked one girl why she liked them and she just said, 'Because they're wicked.' And as she'd obviously been brought up as a Welsh Baptist, you can't blame her for wanting something wicked. She said, 'I've got pictures of Johnny Rotten all over my walls. And Hitler too!' It was rather sweet, really. They're probably all out of work in their sixties by now.

I thought the music was fucking awful. Nothing for me, fuck all. The rhythm section was rotten. It was just amateurish. They were meant to be and they were. I suppose Rotten had stamina, he was able to maintain a paddy for a long time. I just thought it was what teenagers do. It was just standard for a certain age group. The other group – The Clash, I think – were a bit better. I didn't like it, but they were better.

Tom Waits

SINGER, B.1949

I WASN'T that into Tom Waits but I'd heard one record and thought he could write. It was the one with that lyric, 'Small Change got rained on with his own .38.' That line killed me. I didn't go for the voice. What's with the Louis Armstrong? This guy is white.

Assuming that I liked all things Beat – that followed me like an albatross – I was given the job of interviewing him. I don't like all things Beat. I like Burroughs, that one book, *Naked Lunch*. Whoever said about Kerouac, 'That's not writing, that's typing,' I thought had a point. I like bits of Ginsberg. I preferred writers from the Deep South, Faulkner, those cats.

I thought, 'Oh Christ.' Then I looked to see who was in his group and I saw Teddy Edwards was in it. Teddy Edwards! A great tenor player. I said that I'd only do it if they ran a piece on Teddy Edwards as well, seeing as he was in the band. They agreed.

I sat down with Teddy. Christ, hours passed. We ended up exchanging Christmas cards. He was a lovely cat and he told you stuff. You could imagine how it was: that post-war economy, money everywhere, jazz all over the place, playing with Dexter and Wardell Gray. 'Getting the pots on,' he called it. Teddy was terrific, a sweet man. He told me he was dictating all this stuff to one of the big American colleges. He told me they were paying him $10 an hour. 'So far, I've got to the age of three,' he said.

Tom Waits

Anyway, I got to Tom Waits, and it was all right. He was doing the usual hotel room, nothing much, routine, and I wrote it up. Not long after, *NME* said, 'You know Tom Waits, he's doing a show in Copenhagen.' I asked if Teddy Edwards was with them, they said he wasn't. 'Oh fuck,' I thought. Anyway, I was sent out there with old Tom Sheehan – the photographer. We got on well.

We went to see the show. It was Tom Waits with an old-fashioned gas lamp, slouching about and someone making rain sounds. He was doing his stuff. After the show, we went backstage and he was dumped. It was a small audience and he didn't think it had gone very well. We said, 'Come and have a beer with us. Cheer yourself up.' He came with us.

Tom had been around a lot of lowlifes and alcoholics. He told us about one whose hand shook so much he'd take off his tie, wrap it round his fist and put the other end over his shoulder and he'd pulley his drink up to his mouth. He was cheering up. He liked all that.

Then we went to another bar. It was a weird bar. It was a gift to Tom. It was full of short, very chunky Asiatic-looking women in leather jackets. Tough. They were playing pool. We had a drink in there and we couldn't work out what it was. I said to the barman, 'What's with these chicks?' He said, 'It's the lesbian chapter of the Eskimo's Hell's Angels.' You couldn't believe it, could you? What's the chances of bumping into them? Inuit Angels! Anyway, we got out of there and by about 4 in the morning we all fell into our respective beds.

The next morning, I said to Tommy that Tom had kept up that Louis Armstrong voice all the time he was with us. I didn't think it was natural. So we thought we'd see if he'd gone down for his brekker – we'd hide behind the screen and see how he ordered his breakfast. 'He won't put it on for a waiter, let alone a Danish waiter,' we thought. So we hid, and he said in the hoarsest voice yet, 'Two eggs. Sunny side up.' We leapt out and said, 'Oh, Tom.'

I interviewed him a couple of times after. I warmed to his music a bit. I like his 'Waltzing Matilda'. I don't mind *Swordfishtrombones*. The writing, his words, are good. It's that one line, really. The one from

Small Change. I thought, 'Christ, that's fast.' 'Short Change', that's the name of this gangster, 'got rained on', they always get shot in the rain and fall on the ground, 'with his own .38.' That's good, that's fast. Boom, boom, boom.

Brian Case

Brian Case

1937 Born in Deptford,
south-east London, to a Welsh
mother and Irish father. Mother
liked hymns, father liked Irish
rebel songs. Grandfather and
father were both policemen.

1949 Hears jazz for the first
time at his friend Eddie's house.
His older brother Geoff had three records – Earl Bostic's 'Flamingo', one
by Charlie Parker and one
by Stan Getz and the Swedish All Stars, all 78s on the wind-up .

1955 Started going to London clubs like the Florida and the
Flamingo. Buys first jazz record – 'probably hard bop, probably
by Jackie McLean.'

1968 His first novel, *The Users*, is published to enthusiastic reviews.

1971 Started writing about jazz for a new magazine founded by
Charlie Gillett called *Let It Rock*. 'Once you were in print, you could
boost records. Fantastic.' Magazine soon collapsed.

1973 Writes for *Inside London*. Again, it was short-lived, lasting for
three issues. However, during its run Brian gets to watch Duke Ellington
rehearse for a concert he was giving at St Margaret's Church, next to
Westminster Abbey. Leads to job at *NME*.

1974 - 1978 Writes for *NME*, becoming their chief jazz correspondent. Develops a 'souped-up' style to keep pace with the likes of Nick Kent. Also starts writing for *The Observer* and goes on the road with the Sex Pistols on their first UK tour.

1978 - 1986 Joined *Melody Maker* at the request of the new editor Richard Williams. On Williams' departure, jazz featured less and less in the paper, so Brian had to start writing about break-dancing films.

1982 Co-edits *The Illustrated Encyclopaedia of Jazz*.

1986 Co-editor of *The Hip* – a book about 'hipsters, jazz and the Beat generation'.

1986 - 2003 Joins *Time Out*, initially as Film Editor. Goes on to become the influential Books Editor, popularizing James Ellroy and much other noir fiction.

2004 - 2013 Regular freelance contributor for the likes of *The Times* and *Uncut*.

Glossary

The Killer Inside Me Jim Thompson
Pop 1280 Jim Thompson
The Grifters Jim Thompson
Rear Window Cornell Woolrich
The Bride Wore Black Cornell Woolrich
Waltz into Darkness Cornell Woolrich
The Big Heat William P. McGivern
The Night of the Hunter Davis Grubb
The Red Right Hand Joel Townsley Rogers
Pick-Up Charles Willeford
In a Lonely Place Dorothy B Hughes
The Tears of Autumn Charles McCarry
Point Blank Richard Stark
Ask the Parrot Richard Stark
Taste of Fear Margaret Millar
Vanish in an Instant Margaret Millar
Murder in the Madhouse Jonathan Latimer
Strangers on a Train Patricia Highsmith
The Glass Cell Patricia Highsmith
The Postman Always Rings Twice James M.Cain
Double Indemnity James M.Cain
Red Harvest Dashiell Hammett
The Big Clock Kenneth Fearing

FILMS

The Godfather 1&2 Al Pacino
Dog Day Afternoon Al Pacino
Scarface Al Pacino
This Sporting Life Richard Harris
The Field Richard Harris
Unforgiven Richard Harris
Get Carter Michael Caine
The Man Who Would Be King Michael Caine
Pickup on South Street Sam Fuller
Underworld USA Sam Fuller

Acknowledgements

Brian Case would like to thank Jeff Barrett and James Oldham
for developing this idea in the first place and spending many hours
on interviews and transcription, and patience!

He would like to dedicate this book to Mick Collins and his Big Band.
Brian has been going to hear Mick Collins and the Band play at the HG Wells
Centre in Bromley for a decade now on the first Monday of each month.
The band have played to a regular and loyal audience and provided
Brian and others with many hours of big band pleasure.

More recently Mick was diagnosed with cancer and is unable to continue
fronting the band which is being led by Paul and Bill, the trombonists.

He also wants to dedicate the book to his ever growing band of girls:
Sonia, Daisy, Molly, Dotty and the new babe to be.

Conceived by Jeff Barrett and James Oldham
Interviews: James Oldham
Editor: Ian Preece
Design: Lora Findlay
Illustrations: © Joseph Ciardiello
Photo: Brian David Stevens
Printed by: TJ International Ltd, Padstow, Cornwall

Published by *Caught by the River* in 2015.

ISBN 978-0-9572425-2-4

caughtbytheriver.net

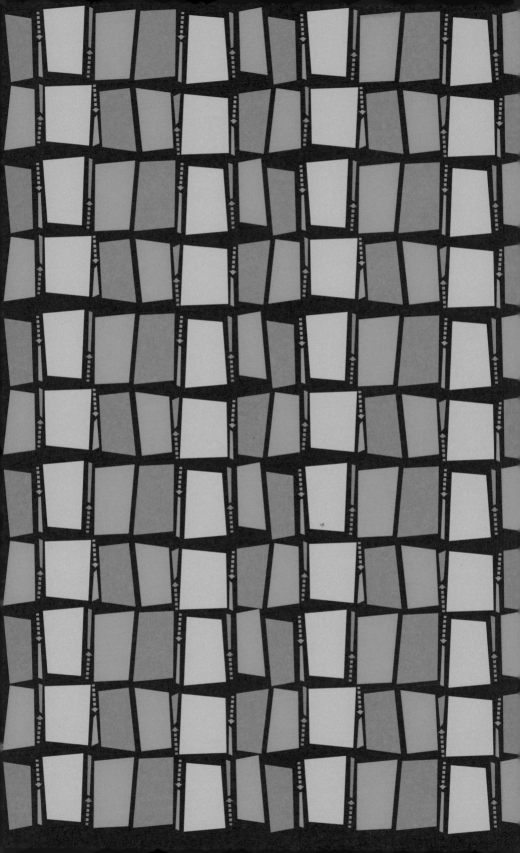